EXPORT BUSINESS

7 STRATEGIC MOVES,

NO BIG EXPORTER IS TALKING ABOUT

BOOSTER

GUIDE FOR MANUFACTURERS

NITIN GUPTA

Worldwide Published by
Pendown Press

PENDOWN PRESS LLP
An ISO 9001 & ISO 14001 Certified Co.,
Regd. Office: 3767A, Kanhaiya Nagar,
Tri Nagar, Delhi-110035
Ph.: 8130886000, 9650072927, 8595249536
E-mail: info@pendownpress.com
Branch Office: 1A/2A, 20, Hari Sadan, Ansari Road,
Daryaganj, New Delhi-110002
Ph.: 011-45794768
Website: PendownPress.com

First Edition: 2023
Price: ₹299/-
ISBN: 978-93-5554-817-7

Layout and Cover Designed by Pendown Graphics Team
Printed and Bound in India by Thomson Press India Ltd.

Contents

My Road To Success

In 1995, I discovered a 3D artwork on a friend's desktop, which sparked my interest in 3D technology. I witnessed the industry's remarkable growth, and as a graduate in interior design, I began working with well-known brands such as Pizza Hut, Dominos, and Barista. However, when I felt there's nothing creative left in my job, I ventured into marketing technology in 2004 and started 'The Next Design'.

Our team successfully completed a project for Bank of America in New York, a massive 20,000-square-foot office, in just 15 days instead of the expected three months. This accomplishment infused me with new energy. Despite my background as a B.Com graduate with no engineering expertise, I took on an oil refinery project, offered to bear 50% of the cost, and delivered it within three months, impressing even the engineers involved.

My journey continued with collaborations, including large corporations such as NTPC and ONGC, Maharatna companies. Projects with BMW, Amazon, Maruti and Kohler India further enriched my experience. Over the course of 20 years, I've had the privilege of working with Fortune 500 companies across diverse industries like aviation, power, and manufacturing, helping them solve their business problems.

This wide range of experience has honed my ability to understand people's challenges and identify where they need assistance. I've become skilled at identifying roadblocks and envisioning how technology can bridge these gaps. Now, my mission is to use my skills and marketing expertise to empower manufacturers, drive their business growth, and help them boost their exports.

By the time you finish this book, I believe you will have a deeper understanding of the dynamic landscape of technology. You will be better equipped to navigate its challenges and ready to seize its opportunities. In the words of Herbert Spencer, "The great aim of education is not knowledge but action." This book represents a tangible step towards action, offering a professional and comprehensive exploration of how technology can be harnessed to drive real-world results.

Overview: The Current Scenario

In the current scenario of the business environment, manufacturers often find themselves in a challenging situation. They invest heavily in participating in exhibitions, setting up large stalls, and meeting both local and foreign buyers with high hopes of getting big orders and expanding their business. While these efforts generate numerous leads and potential opportunities, the problem arises when they struggle to convert these leads into actual orders.

Manufacturers face financial pressure due to loans for equipment purchases or building new factories. Each month, they have to allocate a significant portion of their earnings towards repaying these loans. At the same time, daily expenses and operating costs keep adding up, and as time goes on, waiting for orders to come in becomes increasingly desperate.

Adding to the difficulties, profit margins in the manufacturing industry are usually quite slim, leaving manufacturers with no room for mistakes. This combination of high expenses, loan obligations, and tight margins makes it a tough and sometimes unsustainable situation for manufacturers.

While more established business owners may not face issues with loans and EMI, they might struggle to scale up their business at the desired speed and achieve the high profit margins they want.

Huge investments have been made in building the manufacturing facilities, and most of the visitors who come to these facilities get converted. However, the challenge lies in getting them to the plant itself. A lack of plant visits often translates to lack of new customers!

This book aims to provide valuable guidance and strategies to help manufacturers escape this challenging scenario and transition into a state of better growth and higher profitability. It will explore ways to improve the conversion of leads into actual orders and allow you to include technology in your marketing plan for a 2x growth in the years to come.

PART 01

WHAT MISTAKES ARE YOU MAKING

Chapter 1

5 Mistakes Why People Fail To Convert Leads From International Trade Shows

Trade shows are like finding a treasure chest filled with growth opportunities for your business. However, there are times when, even after collecting lots of leads, we find it tough to turn them into actual orders. In this chapter, we'll talk about five common reasons why this happens. We'll keep it simple and show you how to overcome these hurdles, so you can make the most out of the leads you get at trade shows.

Mistake 1. The Chase of the 3% immediate leads

In business, we often aim for the quickest and most immediate return on investment (ROI), like picking the ripest fruit from a tree. However, the reality is that among all potential leads, only a mere 3% have an immediate need aligned with our offerings, and we can convert just 1% of them.

What complicates matters is that our competitors are also targeting the same 3% of immediate prospects, resulting in a challenging environment for lead conversion.

It's time to shift our perspective. Instead of always wanting instant results, let's focus on a bigger picture – the untapped potential within the remaining 97%. There's a wealth of untapped business waiting to be discovered there, and by focusing on this larger market, we can open doors to new opportunities and achieve 2x growth.

Mistake 2. Not filtering the leads:

Most business owners get lots of business cards during the trade shows. They come back and instruct their sales team to start sending follow-up emails to all of them. However, one size doesn't fit all, and not filtering the leads is a big mistake they make. While big companies may have an organized way of doing this but most small business owners I have spoken to don't know how to do this.

To help you in this process, we have developed a framework for filtering leads at a microscopic level. This strategy allows us to allocate our efforts and resources more efficiently, focusing on the most promising prospects and making the most out of the opportunities we've generated. The lead filtering framework is called BANTEC.

B- Budget: Does the prospect have a budget? "The situation is such that only the person holding the purse strings has the authority to make decisions or issue orders."

A- Authority/Decision maker: Is the prospect the ultimate decision maker (e.g., Managing Director), an influencer (e.g., consultant), or the end user of your product? Identify their role.

N- Need: What is the prospect's specific and urgent problem?

T- Timing: Is the need immediate or in the future? You can plan your marketing activities accordingly.

E- Engagement: Create a 3-star rating to assess the level of engagement with them at the booth. It will help you in personalizing the follow-up email, thereby increasing the conversion rate. The higher the engagement, the hotter the lead is.

C- Competition: Research how your prospect is fulfilling his needs at present. Determine which of your competitors they are purchasing from, and if possible, find out their pricing. There are a lot of websites where you can buy such data. This information will help you in sniper marketing.

You need to segregate your leads with these parameters and then follow up strategically with a focused approach. It will save your time and energy from getting wasted.

When you apply BANTEC framework, here's what you get: 15-20% QUALIFIED LEADS, which is a very good number. Each lead has the potential to generate business in lakhs and crores.

Write down the potential business from one international customer over 5 years.

Write down how many such prospects you have that pass the BANTEC filtration process.

Write down the total potential business that can be harnessed from these filtered leads.

Write down the specific actions you have taken to tap into this business.

Mistake 3. No lead nurturing plan in place

Now that we have seen above the huge business that is lying untapped in the form of unconverted leads, you might want to look at a way to tap this potential business. Just like plants in a garden or a mango farm, business leads also take time to give fruitful results. If we do not nurture these leads, we cannot expect the desired results. When I say 'nurturing leads,' I mean not just maintaining consistent contact with them through phone calls, emails, or text messages; it involves building a valueable relationship. How you keep in touch doesn't matter; what value you add, that matters.

Our current follow-up systems have some shortcomings:

#1. Typically, we send a standard email to all the business cards we receive. Only a few people make the extra effort to craft personalized follow-up emails.

#2. We follow up once or twice, but we lack extended email follow-up sequences. Out of sight is out of mind.

#3. We don't use advanced CRM tools for follow up. They have their own amazing benefits.

#4. Typically, we follow up with the intent of getting orders and not taking the relationship to the next level. Because people buy from people they trust and who add value to their lives.

Ideally, we should be sending them emails or even physical letters (to stand out from the crowd) with valuable information that can be helpful. However, remember that what you find valuable may not necessarily be valuable for them. So, keep that in mind while creating your lead nurturing plan.

Mistake 4. No USP

The customer has so many choices in today's world. The question is, why should they buy from you? They want a solid reason to buy from you, but they can't seem to figure out why. On what criteria can you distinguish yourself? Price and quality are at par with the competition. So, in essence, we lack a compelling reason for them to choose us.

The solution is to create a Unique Selling Proposition (USP) – perhaps your manufacturing facility, your trust-building activities, or maybe the way you are marketing and presenting your business can become your USP? Trust is the basis on which all the business happens globally. So, what can you do to increase your trust level with your prospect? Just some food for thought.

Mistake 5. We don't understand our prospects well enough

Imagine how beneficial it would be if we had a deep understanding of our customers. With such insights, we would find it significantly easier to secure deals by precisely catering to their desires and identifying our precise target audience. Moreover, this knowledge enable us to craft more effective and targeted marketing strategies, ensuring that our efforts are aligned with our customers' needs and desires. The ability to connect on a deeper level with our audience not only enhances our relationship with our customer but also increases our chances for success.

"Goal Karna Hai To Goalkeeper Ke Dimag Par Hamla Karo, Goal Khud-Ba-Khud Ho Jaega."

~Shah Rukh Khan

We need to adopt a similar strategy to reach our goal. Let's study the mind map of our customers for a deeper understanding of their thought process. Only then we will be able to crack the export deals.

Chapter 2

Understanding The Mindset Of The International Buyer

When it comes to international business, understanding the buyer is like having a secret map to success. This chapter is all about decoding how international buyers think and what makes them trust a manufacturer enough to do business. Let's get into it.

- **Manufacturer or Trader**

  When it comes to choosing a supplier, it's essential to know if they are a genuine manufacturer or a trader. This is really crucial because international buyers have burnt their fingers worldwide. Lots of people portray themselves as manufacturers but in reality, are traders.

  To be sure you're a genuine manufacturer, you need to prove at different levels that it's your plant. However, if you're a trader, honesty is the key. You should be transparent about your capabilities and show that you can provide good value for the money.

- ## Production Standards

  The buyer needs a supplier who meets their production standards, ensuring that the product passes their test. Do your products pass global quality standards?

  Because, product quality is non-negotiable; it must be 100%. Without this, you won't stand a chance in the market. Therefore, a high-quality product is a fundamental prerequisite.

- ## Systems and Processes Checklist

  Next, the buyer needs someone with systems, processes, and checklists in place. In case of any rejections, how do you handle them? Do you have documentation explaining what went wrong, why it happened, and the steps you have taken to prevent it from occurring again?

- ## On-Time Delivery

  The most crucial element for any international buyer is timely delivery by the supplier. Delays in delivery disrupt the entire supply chain, leading to huge losses and putting you at risk of potential blacklisting. The entire supply chain, which may involve hundreds or thousands of crores, relies on timely deliveries. Thus, the buyer is looking for a supplier who can guarantee 100% timely delivery.

- ## Production Capacity

  The buyer is concerned about the production capacity of the manufacturer. He wants to make sure that the order size is doable and not beyond his capacity. Typically, people out of greed and desperation, take up larger orders than they can manage and end up in failing in delivery. Thus, your ability to prove your production capacity will work in your favour a great deal.

- **Raw Material Storage, Availability and Labour**

  He wants to find a supplier who has everything needed to complete their orders on time. This includes having the money to buy raw materials, and having a place to store them safely in their factory. Having sufficient and skilled labour is also a big concern, as skilled labour is often scarce in the manufacturing industry.

- **Solid Infrastructure**

  The international buyer needs a supplier who can help when unexpected problems arise. Emergencies happen in every business, and he wants a reliable vendor who can assist in these situations. So, a strong infrastructure is essential to handle this.

- **Response Time**

  For the end customer who is buying your products, the response time is critical. The assembly line just cannot stop. In case of any unexpected situation, the buyers want to have a real-time response ideally. This can be a deal-breaker too. Put yoruself in the shoes of your buyer. If your supplier don't respond fast, isn't he making your life difficult? Would you not like to look for a different supplier in that case? The same is with your buyer too!

- ## Financial Soundness

The manufacturing business is captial-intensive. International buyers look for a financially stable supplier. Many business owners face money problems and have taken loans, which is common worldwide. So, one wants to make sure that his supplier is in good financial shape. Think of ways to communicate that to your buyer.

- ## Past Projects

Prospects place a high value on trust, especially when it comes to choosing a manufacturer. They are more likely to lean towards a manufacturer with a proven track record of delivering orders on time and meeting their expectations consistently. This underscores the significant role that testimonials play in our business. Testimonials provide valuable social proof, showcasing our reliability and the positive experiences of past customers.

- ## In-house Tool Room/Workshop

Off-the-shelf tools enable quick production and reduce the time required for tool development. Meanwhile, an in-house facility offers the flexibility to quickly customize or create specialized tools, minimizing reliance on external suppliers and enhancing adaptability to meet unique customer demands. This combination underscores the manufacturer's commitment to efficiency and customer satisfaction in a competitive manufacturing landscape.

- **Sustainable Practices**

The world is going through climate change, and it will worsen in the years to come. Therefore, sustainability will soon become a standard in global manufacturing practices. Buyers are looking for suppliers who are environmentally sensitive and is following sustainable practices. Are you moving towards sustainable manufacturing?

- **Employee Safety**

In India, factory workers may not always wear safety gear, but for the international companies, the safety of their workforce is of utmost importance. When communicating with your prospects, remember this crucial factor. The more compliance you can demonstrate, the better it is for you and for your workforce safety.

- **Fear**

The person in charge of heading the vendor development team is also an employee. His job is at stake if he brings an incompetent manufacturer on board. Thus, all the factors discussed above are crucial for him and arise from the fear of losing his job. Finding the right and reliable supplier is most important for him. Price is not a concern in his mind; his primary motivation is to safeguard his job. Your job is to alleviate his fears and risks at every stage of communication. If you can achieve that, your export orders will continue to rise.

Chapter 3

Biggest Mistake
that is Costing you Crores

As discussed earlier, all his fears are related to your Infrastructure, be it timely delivery, raw material storage, or support infrastructure for a prompt response in case of any emergency situation. Therefore, your manufacturing plant plays the most significant and decisive role in gaining his trust and securing the order. He's not just picking a supplier; he's putting his job on the line. So, he needs to be 100% sure about your manufacturing facility and infrastructure. Your manufacturing facility is the most important and decisive factor in your lead conversion.

Now that we know how much our international buyer cares about our manufacturing facility, we need to make sure we show it in the best way possible.

Now, let's move forward and see how we are presenting our infrastructure as of today!

- **No Photos:**

  Many manufacturers talk a lot about their plants and size of their factories but often don't show pictures of their actual plant on their website. It's like writing an exciting adventure story without any pictures of the places you've visited. Seeing is believing, and having photos of our plant facility helps people understand what we're really capable of. However, still, regular photos can be manipulated, so that still may be a concern for the buyer. But certainly, something is better than nothing.

- **Small Photos:**

  The images are tiny, like the size of a postage stamp. They don't help convince your dream client about the top-notch quality of your infrastructure.

- **Video Calls:**

  Another way people show their infrastructure is through online video calls, like WhatsApp, Zoom, or Skype. However, network issues can disrupt the call. Imagine having a crucial meeting after a long follow-up, and your network can't support the video. Additionally, during video calls, you're often moving around and showing machines,with lots of noise in the background making it hard for the other person to focus on your critical infrastructure. Imagine someone trying to show you the Taj Mahal over a Zoom call. Do you really think the visual experience on a WhatsApp video call will be exciting enough for you to go and visit the Taj Mahal? Most likely, the answser would be a No. Then how can you expect buyers to get convinced about your production facilities?

- ## Corporate Video:

Most human beings have a desire of giving interviews, getting recorded, and seeing their own photos/videos on the screen (includes TV, Cinema, mobiles). That's where the desire for a corporate video arises in reality. The desire to be recognized. The other reason is that since everyone else has it, we should also get it done. Whether it will help or not is not looked into at all. Corporate videos played on small screens at exhibitions don't usually grab anyone's attention, including yours and the visitors. It's more of a formality and personal satisfaction than a practical tool to help you close your dream order. Another limiting factor with corporate videos is that you can't go back and forth in a video based on your prospect's questions or objections. Which means, when you are answering the questions, you don't have any visual support to back it up.

- ## CCTV cameras:

Some people think CCTV camera footage is sufficient, but it's good for internal safety and control, not for marketing. It's like trying to use a needle where a sword is required.

- ## Professional Photographs:

Some people hire professional photographers to take nice pictures, which is good and a minimum requirement for your marketing. However, you'll soon realize what's lacking in it. Have you heard the quote, "A picture is worth a thousand words"? In order to show the whole factory, you might need 50-100 pictures from different angles. To be able to make sense of all these photos as a single factory unit is almost impossible. They show bits and pieces of the factory and not as a complete factory tour. The visual connectivity is missing when you show too many photos and its difficult to relate as a continuous tour.

- **Drone Video:**

Although drone aerial shots are better than showing eye-level photos, they are still just videos. Morever, the angle of a drone video is also limited. How do you decide which angles to take? On what basis? The other thing is drone videos lack interactivity and may not fully engage the audience. We want to engage the customer as much as possible because more engagement leaves a stronger impression on their mind, increasing the chances of conversion. The third issue with drones is again like the corporate video, you can't go back-and-forth based on the discussion with your prospect. It lacks interactivity.

- **YouTube Videos:**

Sharing YouTube videos of people working may seem generic to clients, making them think you borrowed or stole it from another company. Even showing close-ups of machines and their operation might not be enough to win their trust. Clients might wonder if these machines are truly yours or if you acquired them from somewhere else. This approach may not be as effective in building trust with clients because it doesn't provide a comprehensive view of the manufacturing process or the unique value that sets you apart as a manufacturer.

None of the methods we've talked about so far work well enough. What they really want is to come and see your factory in person. But because of COVID, people have gone into their comfor zones of working from home and are less willing to travel these days as they were in the past. It's been hard to invite people for factory visits, and it's hurting your business. No plant visit typically means no new customers!

So, when we invite them to visit, it takes a long time— 6 to 12 months or even more. The waiting time seems to be endless, and the order remains stuck too.

Another point is when you invite 100 people, typically the plant visit ratio is 1% or less, which essentially means 99% people will not give you business (as they have not seen your plant yet). Orders often don't come until they see our factory, and this hurts our cash flow and growth. Manufacturers have to deal with paying back loans, interest, and other fixed expenses without enough high-profit margin orders. They will not get the growth at the speed and scale that they are looking for.

Have you ever been in a situation like this?

The conversation above emphasizes a big point: Your orders depend on people seeing your factory. Even though it's so important, people often don't showcase it well, and this causes them to lose a lot of business. Many manufacturers make this mistake, having great facilities but not prensenting in a effective way that builds trust with new prospects instantly.

Chapter 4

Core Reason For Low Margins

Manufacturers work hard, day and night, and give their best to thei rbusiness. They build a brand image in the market, which they feel is good. But, that "good" is their perception. In many cases, it is not good enough in the eyes of the clients. If the clients perceived them as a premium brand, their story would have been different today.

Let me share a short story with you. I have a background in interior design, and 16 years ago, I designed my own office in a basement. My online marketing efforts led to a client in the US who came to meet me in Delhi. When I took him to my office (I was really excited about my design), he took some photos. My excitement grew, and I asked him, 'Why are you taking pictures?' He said, 'I want to show my colleagues in the US, who are complaining about the office interiors, that people work in such small offices too.' It was a reality check for me. The point I want to make is that it's all about perception. Your audience may not see you the way you see yourself. Prospects don't immediately visit your factory; they see your website, catalogs, trade show booth, product visuals, and how you present yourself, among other things. This creates the first impression.

People who meet you at your trade show typically go back and visit your website and LinkedIn profile. We, as human beings, are conditioned to pay a higher price for a brand that appears premium and more reliable. A premium brand does business with higher profit margins.

I wish manufacturers paid the same attention and spent the same amount of money as they invest in their cars, electronic gadgets, clothes and homes. When it comes to building a new home or renovating your home, your wallets and mindset are wide open. However, when it comes to investing in best marketing collaterals, everything suddenly starts appearing expensive. Did you just smile? :-) If you want to rise above 'vendor-vendor' and 'price-price' game, you have no choice but to look like a top-quality and trusted brand. Just food for thought!

I often quote this to my audience, *"Sasta Dikhega, toh Sasta Bikega."*

PART 02

WHAT CAN WE DO ABOUT THEM?

Chapter 5

7 Essential Strategies To Elevate Your Brand Image & Get New Export Orders

Now that we've talked about the situation and the mistakes you as a manufacturer often make, it's time to use technology wisely to improve things. In this part, we'll look at seven specific strategies that can make your brand look premium, increase your profit margins, and bring in a lot of new international customers. They're strategic moves that will make your marketing efforts more effective and help you succeed.

World-class manufacturing companies around the world adopt these seven strategies.

Strategy 1: Let your Factory do the talking

As discussed earlier, the decisive factor in your business is your plant and infrastructure. If you are not presenting your plant in the most effective & influential manner then you are losing huge potential business. Showing your complete factories interactively goes a long way in building instant trust with your buyer, removing his objections, and can help you secure more orders.

The magical solution lies in the cutting-edge technology called VPV (Virtual Plant Visit).

VPV is an immersive technology based on the Instant Trust Building Framework, that creates a holistic digital experience that allows users to explore and interact with your manufacturing facility. It provides a simulated, immersive experience that closely replicates being physically present at the plant.

This cutting-edge technology is set to make your marketing efforts more effective and increase your conversion ratio by at least 50% by way of building Instant Trust with the international buyers.

Benefits of VPV

1. **Instant Trust Building (ITB):** In the past decade, international buyers have been often cheated by individuals who falsely claimed to be manufacturers and then failed to deliver on their promises. Their fraudulent intentions and actions have created a widespread mistrust in the entire export industry. Trust is hard to come by these days, but VPV has all the components needed to quickly build trust, automatically opening doors for your business.

2. **Stand Out from Traders:** As mentioned earlier, some traders make websites and portray themselves as manufacturers. This comprehensive solution helps you stand out from the league of these traders. This is not meant to demean traders, as they play an important role in the industry. However, international buyers generally prefer to deal with manufacturers directly. That's it!

3. **Differentiate from Your Competition:** The manufacturing world is full of competition, no matter what you produce. Since the product is a commodity you must find other ways of differentiating from your competitors. VPV can help you stand out and gain an edge over your competitors. While your product and your factory are important, how you present them is equally, if not more, important.

4. **Boost Customer Engagement by 10x:** In today's fast-paced world, capturing and retaining customer attention is a mega challenge. The cost of losing your potential customers is often higher than the cost of production and marketing combined. Participating in international trade shows requires a significant investment of time, money, and energy. Now, once you have captured someone's attention, the more you engage them, the closer you get to cracking the order. VPV helps you engage your customers at a 10x higher level at the trade show.

5. **Better Negotiating Power:** During price negotiations, you may often hear phrases like, "aapka price jyada hai, market me to itne mein milta hai" ("You are charging more; this product is available in the market at a lower price"). You may be having your plant in 5 acres and having a huge team. Still, your customer will never consider that. Clients tend to focus on offering a lower price without taking these factors into account. How can you change this? Use VPV to get the maximum advantage by demonstrating that you can offer after-sales support

and guarantee timely delivery. Lower quotes from the other companies may signify lower expenses and a lack of infrastructure at their end. Now, In reality, your client also wants to play it safe and opt for a supplier who can ensure 100% on-time delivery. By showcasing your plant in detail using VPV, you can influence their subconscious mind and remove the fear regarding quality management and on-time delivery. This, in turn, allows you to negotiate for a better price and more favorable terms and conditions as per your desire.

6. **You move one step forward in closing the deal:** Every order has some gestation period and stages to go through. Once your product passes all the tests, the next step is the plant visit. Demonstrating your manufacturing capabilities and infrastructure using VPV will allow you to address all their objections about production capacity, raw materials, and on-time delivery which are crucial concerns for any buyer, over a zoom call.

7. **Get Shortlisted and stay at the top of the shortlisted contenders for the order:** When your sample gets approved, there is a possibility that samples from other competitors have also been approved. However, no one has seen anyone's plant yet. If you can show your plant in full detail over a Zoom call, won't they place you at the top of the list as they have not seen the manufacturing facility of other competitors?

8. **No need to wait for the prospect to visit the plant:** Typically, a serious buyer who met you at the trade show

would take nothing less than a few months to plan a visit to your plant. Sometimes, this plant visit takes place after dozens of follow-ups and waiting for 6-12 months or even longer. No plant visit means no order. Therefore, you should embrace this technology to reduce your sales cycle. Once you have gained trust through digital mediums, you can ask for a small initial order. Delivering this small order surely eliminates the need for a physical plant visit.

Though physical plant visits are welcomed, but they have three big drawbacks:

a. The time it takes is often too long, leading to reduced cash flow for you.

b. Only a limited number of serious buyers visit the plant, while the rest of the leads may not fully understand your manufacturing capabilities. Which means crores of potential business is lying untapped in the business cards.

c. The third and most important one is that during a plant visit, the buyer may also visit 10 other competitors. Therefore, it makes more more sense to build trust using technology and keep the buyer away until you have delivered the small order. This may not be true if you are having one of the largest plants in Asia.

9. **Get quick decisions from stakeholders worldwide:** Every order involves numerous stakeholders. If the vendor development team has reviewed your plant

virtually using VPV, and their boss is traveling, they can share it with the final decision-makers as a link, securing instant approval for your test order.

10. **Ensures business continuity during lockdowns:** In today's world, we've seen the possibility of lockdowns due to factors like COVID variants or climate-related events such as floods and droughts. If the government announces another lockdown, how will you attract potential buyers to visit your factory? With VPV, you can ensure a smooth virtual plant visits and lead conversion over Zoom calls.

11. **Cost-Effective expansion of dealers worldwide:** Expanding your network of dealers across India can be an expensive endeavor. However, with VPV, you can onboard dealers from all over the world without the need to invest millions in offline virtual plant visits. Dealers give great importance to partnering with strong companies that have a robust manufacturing and support infrastructure. They seek assurance that the company can effectively address any issues that may arise with end consumers. This mutual trust is vital for maintaining healthy relationships between dealers and manufacturers. Introducing VPV plays a pivotal role in addressing these concerns by offering transparent insights into the company's manufacturing capabilities and support systems, thereby bolstering the confidence of both dealers and companies.

12. **Spending lakhs in Travel allowance of Sales team challenge in manufacturing:** In the current scenario, manufacturers face a significant challenge when relying on their sales teams to constantly persuade prospects to come and visit their factory, resulting in substantial conveyance allowances. On average, one salesperson incurs approximately 50,000 rupees in travel allowance per month. When you multiply this by 12, it amounts to 6,00,000 rupees per salesperson per year. If you have a team of ten salespeople, you could be spending a significant 50 to 60 Lakh rupees on sales allowances annually. For an international sales team, this number would be significantly higher.

    However, with the introduction of VPV, you can save lakhs of rupees every month. By giving presentations over Zoom and remotely showcasing your manufacturing plants, you can offer a highly effective and cost-efficient alternative to maintaining large, expensive sales teams. This one-time investment in technology not only enhances your client engagement but also leads to substantial long-term savings, making it a smart and strategic choice for your business.

13. **Show yourself as a big fish:** Manufacturers should work towards consolidation and portraying themselves as a big fish. When they start their business as a manufacturer, they often start with a small factory. As they grow organically, they acquire nearby plots and sometimes end up with 4-5 small buildings in different locations, failing

to represent themselves as big players. While having a large infrastructure matters, if you cannot present yourself in the same manner, you may lose the battle. International buyers are looking for a big manufacturer for the long run. They would not want to be associated with a small-time manufacturer who may not be able to fulfill their growing needs.

14. **Solve the language problem:** Non-English speaking countries such as Japan and Korea are big importers. Marketing your products to such countries could be a challenge due to language barriers. A translator is requried to communicate between both parties. VPV can solve this problem, and you can have a tour created in their native languages discussing their pain points and how you can solve them. Won't that be wonderful? You are not dependent on anyone now to present your company to buyers in such countries?

Strategy 2: Make Your Website Engaging

Most websites I've come across are outdated and don't work well on mobile devices. The text is often too much, and the pictures are of poor quality and too small. The impression your website creates plays a significant role in building your credibility as a quality manufacturer. Quality should be evident in every aspect of your online and offline presence.

1. **Responsive Website:** Your website should be responsive and work properly on both mobile devices and desktops. The most common platform these days to achieve this

is Wordpress. It is a free, open-source content management system (CMS) that allows you to create and manage websites and blogs. It's one of the most popular and widely used CMS platforms on the internet. With WordPress, you can easily create, edit, and organize digital content, making it a versatile tool for building websites, from simple blogs to complex e-commerce sites.

2. **Engaging Visual Content:** Consider using high-quality visuals and interactive ways of presenting your products and factories on your website. Some of the ways to show your products in an engaging format are high-quality 3D product visuals, 360-degree product rotations, and exploded 3D Views. For an immersive factory experience, you can opt for Virtual plant visit, explained above.

a. **Use 3D Product visuals:** Your entire business revolves around your products, and that is one of its weakest links. When people visit your website, they rely on your product visuals, creating a first impression in their minds. If these visuals are not world-class, how can you claim to be a world-class manufacturer and exporter? Ideally, you should show your product as a hero.

It's a big challenge for the manufacturers. Despite having products of international standards, they often find themselves perceived as local players, and, of course, they are compensated accordingly.

The core reason behind this is their inability to portray themselves as premium quality manufacturers. When it comes to premium quality, 3D visuals are a game-changer. Unlike traditional photography, there's no need to worry about shipping your products to photo studios, saving you from logistical headaches. With 3D visuals, you can showcase your products with the highest quality finishing and perfection. These visuals are powerful tools for creating eye-catching and unique communications that help your brand stand out in the crowd. International companies are already using 3D Visuals to showcase themselves as premium brand on their website.

The below 3D visual is an example from an International manufacturing company and is covering 90% of the screen. Big visuals make a bigger impact!

b. **360-degree rotation:** A 360-degree product rotation, also known as a 360-degree view or 360-degree spin, is a digital representation of a product that allows viewers to interactively see the item from all angles.

It's made by taking lots of pictures as the product turns in a full circle. These images are then stitched together to create an interactive visual that viewers can manipulate by dragging or clicking.

c. **Exploded 3D Views:** Exploded 3D views are representations that visually depict the individual components or parts of a complex assembly, machine, or object. In an exploded view, the components are deliberately separated or "exploded" from their normal positions, creating space between them while maintaining their relative spatial relationships. It allows viewers to clearly see each component of a complex structure or device, making it easier to understand how the parts fit together. Overall, exploded 3D views provide a visual way to simplify complex structures and improve communication for buyers.

Strategy 3: Use Exhibitions as the Foundation of Building Trust

The trade show booth should feature a clean design with communication that interests your buyers and solves their pain points. Often, photographed visuals, when enlarged, become pixelated. Make sure you have crisp, sharp visuals, and the marketing message and works as a magnet to attract the right audience to your booth.

Participating and getting more ROI from trade shows can be divided into these 5 categories:

1. **Prepare:** What is your goal from the trade show? Who specifically is your target audience? What is their pain point you intend to solve with your product. Build your marketing collaterals around these.

2. **Attract:** Why should they even look at your booth? Is there a single prominent reason for them to walk towards your booth? Have communication that addresses their pain areas so that they can see relevance in having a conversation with you.

3. **Engage:** Once the visitor is in your booth, the job here is to build a one-to-one relationship with them. Talk about their pain points and don't try to sell your products at this stage. Everybody wants to sell; try to solve their pain areas and see the magic.

4. **Build Trust:** On a trade show booth, you only get one chance to be in a physical meeting with your prospect. This one-to-one meeting should be maximized to build trust. Building trust remotely is extremely difficult and challenging, resulting in loss of business. Educating your customers is a great way to build trust. Selling becomes an automatic byproduct when trust is established through education.

5. **Follow up/Build relationship:** Mostly, big orders take time to manifest. In exports, its follow-up or fail! The relationship you build with your prospect will determine your chances of winning the order. The product, of course, needs to be top quality; that's a given.

Strategy 4:. Create a Lead Nurturing Plan

After the exhibition, people get lots of business cards. The next job is to filter the leads using BANTEC framework discussed above in Part 1. Once you have the filtered leads that need your attention, you need to create a lead nurturing plan. The plan should not just be a series of emails sending company profiles and asking for business. The goal is to add value to the life of your prospects and build a relationship with them using different modes of communication.

It could be a series of emails that provide value to your customers or webinars focused on giving value to your customers. For example:

1. You can talk about the trends in their industry.
2. Point out common mistakes they might be making and how much those mistakes could be costing them.
3. Highlight any malpractices within your industry that customers should be aware of.
4. Share consumer insights that can benefit them.
5. Inform buyers about important exhibitions and events in their field.
6. Check their websites and see if you can find any errors there.

Basically, your intent should be helping your prospect. Yes, it takes some effort and time to create good content, but it's well worth it! When you provide helpful information, it builds trust and shows that you know your stuff. In the long run, the effort you put into creating useful content pays off by connecting you with your more customer at a deeper level. Do Marketing first and then do sales.

After the expo, you should input the business cards data into a CRM. There are hundreds of CRM software options like Zoho, Salesforce, etc. With the help of these tools, you can make a list of people, schedule emails for them like a newsletter, and can also check who has opened the emails and how many times. If a person frequently opens your email, it's a sign of interest, and your sales team can follow up with him accordingly.

Another benefit of CRM is the ability to set up email sequences. For example, if a person opens the first email, then CRM will automatically send the second email that you've prepared. While it does require effort, you don't have to handle all of this on your own. There are CRM teams who can take your voice notes and written ideas and effectively communicate on your behalf.

Strategy 5. Use Smart Catalogue Technology

Using smart catalog technology, we can create an unforgettable experience for your customers. You can create an application with all your product details and a 3D experience of your product and reduce the need to print catalogs and save lakhs of rupees every year.

Your products will be modelled in 3D with the same materials, finishes, and everything else. Your clients can experience your products on their own tables, allowing them to view, rotate, zoom in, zoom out —just like they're holding the product in their hands. This is made possible through Web AR or any other AR applications.

Web AR is basically web-based augmented reality, eliminating the need to create a separate application. You can add a button on your website to enable customers to experience your products in AR. So, when they click this button on their mobile phones, it scans a surface, and your product appears as a 3D model with its finishes, looking very realistic. This technology provides a competitive edge, and very few companies globally are currently implementing it, so you could become one of the early leaders in this exciting field.

Strategy 6: Create a Virtual Showroom

The product that you are manufacturing is a commodity. There is no special distintive feature about it. You must have made 100 different products so far in your journey. How do you show them? Imagine if you can have a virtual showroom where you show all the products you make, will that not set you apart from your competitors in some way? Everyone shows product photos in PDFs, and you show a virtual showroom. Will it not portray you as an innovative and high-tech company?

Strategy 7: Focus on Marketing Instead of Selling

The whole world is trying to sell, sell, and sell. If products could be sold just by selling, the world would be different, and manufacturers would be on cloud 9. For some reason, the focus has always been on selling instead of marketing. Your focus should be on your customer needs and desires instead of just selling your products. If you can build an environment that builds trust and positions you as their best choice, they would certainly buy from you, no questions asked!

Have you ever seen a Starbucks salesperson coming to you and selling coffee? Have you seen Decathlon staff approaching you and pushing you to buy their products? No!

They have identified and segmented their target audience very well. They know everyone is not their customer. They let their visitors engage with their product, their environment. They never push you to buy their products. Have you segmented your audience? Have you thought of ways of engaging your audience so that sales become an automatic by-product of the marketing efforts?

You might want to read a spectacular book called "Purple cow" by Seth Godin. It'll surely have a lot of light bulb moments for you.

We all have been reading and hearing this phrase "sales and marketing". The irony is that Starbucks is doing marketing first and then sales (that too only at the counter level as an upsell). So, get your sequence right. First Marketing, then Sales!!!

PART 03

WHY DO YOU NEED TO TAKE QUICK ACTION?

Chapter 6

The Significance Need
For Embracing Technology, Quickly!

The world is highly dynamic. We've witnessed pioneers like Nokia, Kodak, Blackberry, Xerox drowning in the new waves of technology. Riding the wave that comes with speed and force is a daunting task.

If you don't have the vision, preparation, mindset, and the speed of implementation, you are digging your own grave without even realizing it.

Those who ride this wave will be recognized as leaders, while those who lag in implementation will be thrown out of the window by the fast implementers.

Chapter 7

Three Game-Changing Strategies That Helped Companies Achieve Top-10 Worldwide Status

Let's analyse what the top companies are doing. How were they able to beat their competition and reach the top?

Company	Sector	Market Cap (in USD)
#1 Apple	Technology	$2.744 trillion
#2 Microsoft	Technology	$$2.353 trillion
#3 Saudi Aramco	Oil & Gas	$2.224 trillion
#4 Alphabet (Google)	Technology	$1.624 trillion
#5 Amazon	E-commerce	$1.336 trillion
#6 Nvidia	Technology	$1.069 trillion
#7 Berkshire Hathaway	Diversified Investments	$770.43 billion
#8 Meta Platforms	Social Media	$725.89 billion
#9 Tesla	Automotive	$682.99 billion
#10 Eli Lilly	Pharmaceuticals	$518.71 billion

Global Top 10 Companies by Market Capitalization (Data from Forbes INDIA, Aug 21, 2023)

3 Fundamental elements are working behind the scenes.

1. We are visual beings. We imagine visually, remember visually, and learn visually, for the most part.

2. We like to interact, so companies created smartphones with interactivity.

3. Convenience is the bedrock upon which the whole economy is running- making things convenient for people.

Based on these insights, we have formulated 3 marketing strategies that can change the game, just like them:

Strategy 1: Focus on Visuals

Before getting into it, take this exercise:

Imagine a natural landscape and write down here, what came into your mind- a picture or words?

Recall your happiest memory and write down here, what came into your mind- a picture or words?

What did you have in breakfast today, and write down here, what came into your mind- a picture or words?

This exercise will come in handy as we discuss this terrific Visual Marketing Strategy ahead.

Apple experienced remarkable growth over the past decade. We all are very well aware of the story of Steve Jobs and how he started Apple in a garage. The Apple empire is not a miracle but a result of precise marketing strategy. Why they have always focused on the quality of visuals, user experience, and simplicity? Because those are the fundamentals!

In 2007, the first iPhone was launched, and you can see the compounding growth ever since.

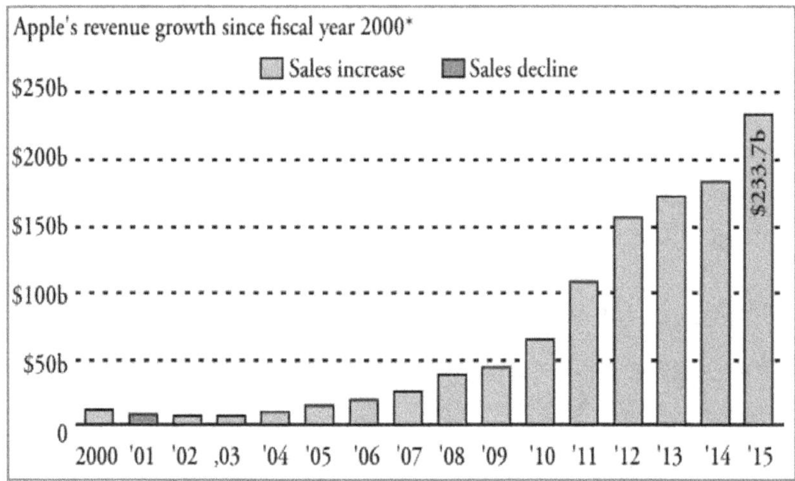

Now is a good time to recall the above exercise. When I asked you to imagine a natural landscape, you would have pictured trees, grasslands, lakes etc. Note that I wrote 'PICTURED.' It wasn't text or sound; it was visuals. We think and imagine in the form of pictures because we are visual beings. Visuals stick to our mind. They create the first impression.

How is this relevant for manufacturers like you?

Our brain processes the visual and categorizes it as a local product or a premium product within a few milliseconds. Now, think about how you present your products. Most of us have commodity products. They may not be visually appealing, and, on top of that, our visuals are not appealing either. You can imagine its impact, or do I need to tell you that?

You have been dependent on photography so far. You ship your products, take all the logistic headaches, packing and unpacking, and also risk the possibility of transportation damage. We simply hope that it arrives at the studio in the same condition in which it was packed, as any damage during transit would be a significant concern.

One thing to consider is that photography can only picturise reality. It cannot beautify your product. All you'll have is a high-resolution photo of your product with details, including product imperfections, stains and scratches.

No doubt it can be fixed, and it is still a widely accepted method for showcasing products, but ask yourself, does it make you stand out and look world class? Does it help you in looking like a premium and quality conscious brand?

No! It's quite the reason even Apple doesn't use product photoshoots for their marketing.

Actionable items for you:

You can evaluate your current visuals in the following areas:

1. Website

2. Catalogs

3. Dealer Showrooms

4. Social Media Communication

5. Your Office

6. Trade Shows

Are there any other areas that you can think of?

____

____

Strategy 2: Focus on Interactivity

All of us switched to the touch screen smartphones from keypad phones. Weren't the older phones good enough for calling and texting? The smartphone brought Android apps, games, social media platforms, and we all adopted them so quickly. And it wasn't just adoption; they became an inseparable part of our lives. Ever wondered why?

As human beings, we love to 'interact.' When visuals become interactive visuals, they become amusing, something that can grasp anyone's attention. The interactive registers in our minds even better than visuals.

Take the example of NVIDIA & Meta Platforms:

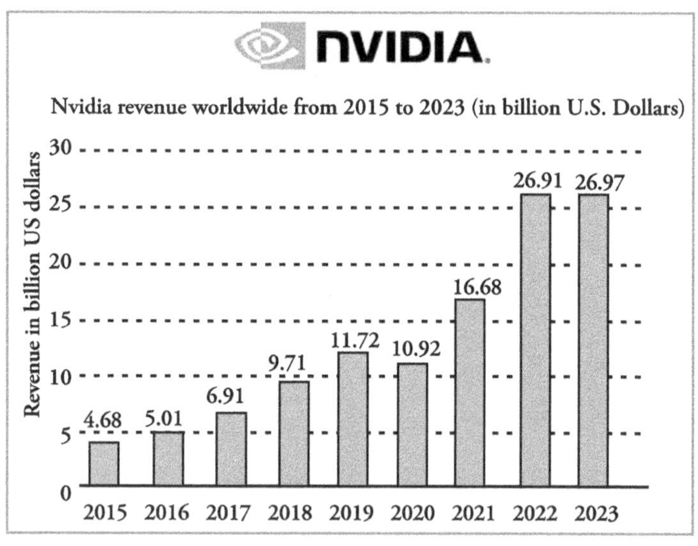

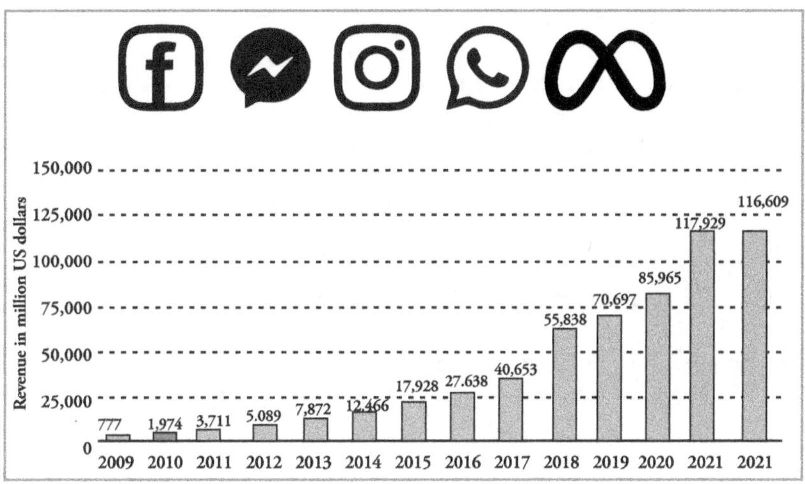

Using interactivity strategically can bring about a significant change in your ROI, as evident in the graphs shown above. Both are the leading companies in the field of interactive business.

Interactive tools serve as more than just attention-grabbers; they can serve as a unique selling proposition (USP) for your business. By embracing interactive marketing technologies, you can engage your prospects for longer durations and build more trust online. In such a competitive world where the customer has 100 options to choose from, it is important for you to be in the consideration list, to be in his mind as a possible option. Using interactive product techniques, you can explain your product features better. Using interactive factory tours such as VPV, you can address all their objections regarding production capacity, timely delivery, etc., in an interactive virtual factory tour. They not only engage your audience but also set you apart as an innovative and customer-centric entity, which is increasingly valuable in a competitive market.

Actionable items for you:

1. Create interactive product demonstrations online.

2. Create interactive virtual plant visits.

3. Create interactive dealer displays. (may be touch screen displays?)

4. Create interactive smart catalogs.

5. Interact more with your customers as Interactions between you and your customers also fall under Interactivity. Look at the word "Interactivity"; it has the word "Interact" in-built. Which means the fundamental theme behind interactivity is to intearact with your customer.

6. Other areas you can think of increasing interaction with your customers:

____

____

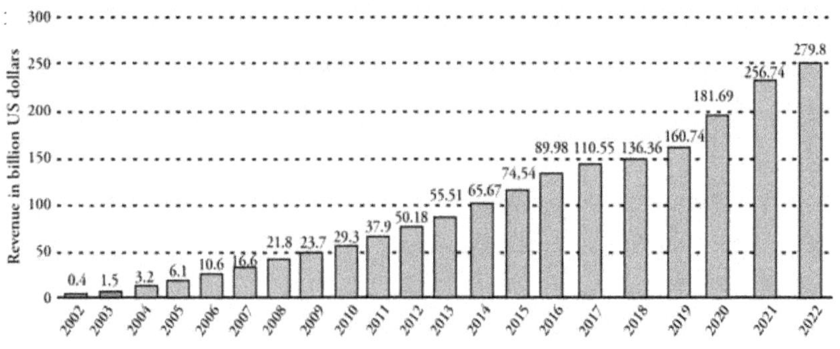

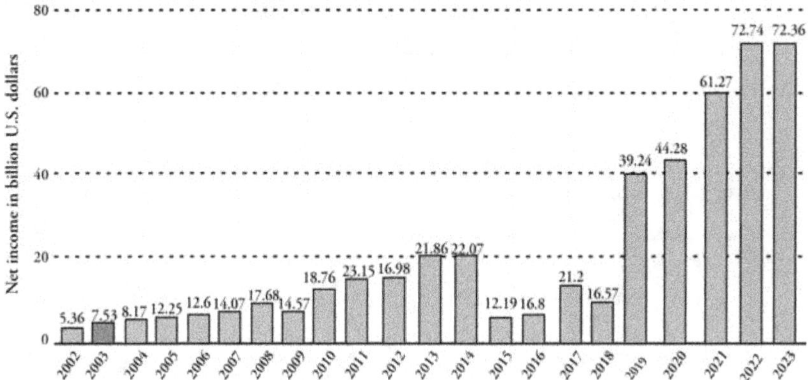

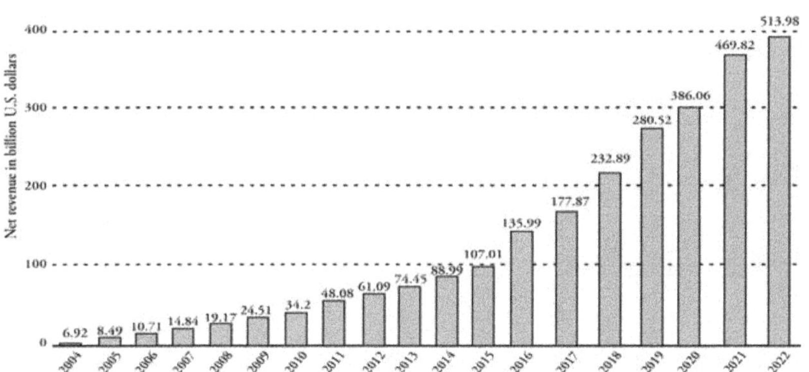

Certainly, we all appreciate the value of convenience, both as buyers or in our daily lives. Companies like Amazon, Google, and Microsoft have excelled in understanding this concept.

Microsoft offers technology that simplifies work, Google provides answers to our questions, YouTube offers a wealth of video content that makes our life convenient, and Amazon delivers products right to your doorstep, even handling returns seamlessly. In today's fast-paced era, just a few clicks can accomplish so much.

Here are some areas where you can incorporate convenience:

1. Learning the local language, if your buyer is from a non-English speaking country.

2. Plant visit: Because of COVID, people have become accustomed to working from home and prefer to travel less and less. Go for Interactive Virtual Plant Visit.

3. Can you open your new manufacturing plant near your customer's plant?

4. Can you offer them real-time order tracking system?

5. Can you give them a single point of contact for all their queries?

6. Any other ideas you can think of?

____

____

____

____

When it comes to plant visits, we often want buyers to travel in person, which may not be convenient for foreign buyers visiting another country. Sometimes, it's a team of people who come, requiring significant coordination and scheduling. This potential inconvenience could be a challenge. Moreover, in today's competitive landscape, offering convenience in this aspect can be a game-changer. Just as we seek convenience, our buyers also appreciate it, and being able to provide it could set us apart in a highly competitive market.

PART 04

WHEN YOU WILL START IMPLEMENTATION, YOU WILL FACE OBSTACLES

Chapter 8

7 Roadblocks in Your Business Expansion

7 Roadblocks in Your Business Expansion

1. Oh, I already know this!

"Oh, I already know this. I've seen this." It's good that you have seen it. But the game lies in implementation. In today's tech-dominated world, we all know a lot of things. We all know that yoga and meditation are essential for a healthy life. But how many of us actually practice them regularly?

2. Procrastination:

We Procrastinate, often saying, 'I will do it later, first this...

Procrastination is a common challenge that many of us face when it comes to implementing new ideas or making changes in our lives. We often delay taking action because of internal doubts and uncertainties. This procrastination stems from our hesitation to make decisions without a guarantee of success. As humans, we fear making wrong choices and appearing foolish. Therefore, we tend to put off trying something new and opt for the familiar instead.

51

However, hesitating to embrace the latest marketing technologies leads to significant barriers in our progress.

Why Do We Procrastinate?

i. **Fear of failure:** Our conditioning has been such that failure is considered bad. "He failed!!!!" What a taboo it is in our society. That has been ingrained in our minds for generations. We don't want to fail because society will look down upon us. Thus, we don't want to try anything that has a probability of failure. We want guaranteed success! If someone can give us a guarantee, we are willing to take action. There is no guarantee that we'll wake up tomorrow morning, and yet, we expect a guarantee for new things we try? This fear of failure is one of the main reasons why we procrastinate. I would urge you to dig deep inside yourself and see if you can relate to it.

ii. **Belief Systems:** Doubts and belief systems play a significant role in our reluctance to embrace change or pursue new endeavours. We often tell ourselves that we are not capable of certain tasks, especially in the tech-dominated world. Thoughts like, "I am not a tech person," or "This is too tough for me to implement," hold us back. It is ONLY AND ONLY OUR BELIEF SYSTEM that drives our lives, let alone business growth.

iii. **Doubts:** We also question the viability of our ideas and investments, wondering if they will truly work or if anyone else has succeeded in similar ventures. Doubts about the worthiness of our investments in marketing endeavors further contribute to our hesitation. Whether it will work or not! Will I be able to do it or not? He has gone to IIT, IIM, I haven't, and all other sorts of baseless reasons come to our minds. And these reasons don't allow you to take action. And no action means no result. The same action means the same result.

iv. Past experiences: It did not work in the past with someone I know or when I tried it last time, it didn't work. So, we conclude that it doesn't work, and we procrastinate. We have become very judgemental and jump to conclusions very fast. It's all pre-conditioned in our minds, and our judgements come automatically. The right thing to do is to ask the right question. The right question is "Why it didn't work? Dig into that reason.

3. Your Fundamentals:

Behind any success, be it a successful movie or a successful business, fundamentals play an   important role. However, in the context of manufacturing, you have to get your hands dirty, engage in on-the-ground execution, and face challenges. You might stumble and fall, learn from your experiences, and get back on your feet. This cycle keeps repeating. We frequently seek advice from our friends and family, but do they really have the right expertise and knowledge to guide you?

The question here is, how do we know if our fundamental ways of working are correct? How do we determine if our fundamentals are right? If your fundamentals are correct, your graph would be up and up.

Consider the progress you have already achieved independently. Now, envision the potential for even more remarkable results when equipped with the appropriate guidance and support. Certainly, if you are open to learning and bringing in the right consultant to your company, you can avoid costly mistakes and save time and money. In today's world, we must identify champions in each area of our lives.

For example: A fitness coach, a marketing coach, a lawyer, a doctor, and so on. Instead of trying and failing on our own, it's best to hire professionals to get your job done the right way and more efficiently.

4. Lack of "Proper" Implementation:

We have been born and brought up in an environment where money is perceived as a scarce resource. A person who has Rs.10,000/- in his bank is insecure, and a person who has 100 crores in his bank is also insecure (definitely 100 times more). This leads to our inclination to save money, and more often than not, we end up taking the "cheaper route" when it comes to investing in marketing collateral. "Oh, this is so expensive!". Now, you have implemented what you needed to, but not in the best manner. You get what you pay for, and the results suffer.

The interesting thing is that we have money in our banks to invest; it is our mindset that stops us and pushes us to go for the cheaper routes which leads to compromise in quality and the devaluation of your brand.

5. Desperation:

There is also an element of "Immediate results" in our minds. You need to be aware of that too. All good things take time to build, and all good results take time to show up. The world of instant delivery is conditioning our minds in a negative way.

6. Lack of Attention to Details:

We often don't dig into why things didn't work. I have seen people participating in multiple exhibitions in a year, spending millions and millions in these trade shows. Each trade show leading to lots of business cards and leads. If we properly work on them, we really don't need to participate in so many trade shows. Unfortunately, we often don't get into the details of why the leads are not converting.

7. Comfort Zone:

Who doesn't want to grow? But when you dig deep down, many people become complacent. With enough money in their bank and people working for them, nothing much will happen if sales dip a bit or there is no growth. The fire is not there which used to be when you started the business. Complacency takes over. I am not saying you are complacent, but it's a point that can't be ignored when you are introspecting.

In any area of your life, achieving desired results requires a lot of hard work. We often put in hard work in the areas we love and where we are strong. Going out of your comfort zone and doing hard work is what is required, and it's only done by very few. Those who do it can be seen as the top players in any industry.

The key to remove the roadblocks is to SHIFT YOUR VIEWPOINT: Go fearless and embrace the fear of failure/ rejection.

Rather than seeking a guarantee of success, you should consider trying fast and failing fast. Learn the lessons and move forward faster. Also, consider this: by the time you figure out that it works, you lose the early-start advantage, and you may have missed out on valuable opportunities. Even the government doesn't guarantee the whole amount in our bank, but our mind demands guarantees everywhere.

In a fast-paced, tech-driven world, doubts, procrastination, and rigid beliefs can hold us back. In order to succeed, you need to embrace uncertainty and see value in partial success and lessons learnt. I want to emphasize the importance of considering these technologies as investments rather than expenses. While no tool or strategy can promise absolute and direct success, the incremental improvements these technologies offer help you get closer and closer to your desired outcome. Act now to unlock opportunities and avoid missing out.

PART 05

THE FUNDAMENTAL REASON WHY PEOPLE STAGNATE

Chapter 9

The Fundamental Reason Why People Stagnate

Stagnation occurs because we often find ourselves doing the same thing again and again, with no change in the equation. In fact, if you go deep, you'll realize that we've been stuck in this cycle for many lifetimes! If you do not believe in spirituality, you can consider that we've been repeating the same actions for many years. Yet, we wonder why we are not getting the results we desire.

For example:

$9+9 = 18$

$9+9 = 18$

$9+9 = 18$

However, if you **think creatively,** you can simply twist the "+" sign 45 degrees, and the equation changes to:

$9 \times 9 = 81$

Did you notice that a massive result can be achieved by making the right change in equation?

So, what are the possible changes in the equation?

Change in Product

Most manufacturers have made heavy investments in plant and machinery, and the capital investment is significant. The product is often a commodity with specifications defined by the customer. It's challenging to change the product, but not impossible. However, if you can make that change, you can achieve great results.

Change in Customers/Market/Geography

After speaking to hundreds of manufacturers, it is evident that in the quest to increase volumes, many business owners work with anybody and everybody, often accepting low-profit margins. Later, they regret when those orders result in almost negligible profits and consume a significant amount of their energy, making their lives like a hell. In such cases, exploring the export market can be a game-changer. Of course, it's tough, but you may want to look at the possibility of changing the equation here.

Change in Delivery

Dominos is a great example that focuses on On-time Delivery. No other player in the market has positioned itself so strongly with on-time delivery as its one of the primary bases. Another example is Netflix. Netflix used to be in the business of renting cassettes. They then transitioned it to renting out the DVDs. They further evolved by adopting a monthly subscription model, shifting their delivery method from offline to online subscription-based content. This change aligns with the current needs of the hour. The world is changing faster than at any other time in human history. Do you think you can add a process or team to make sure you can deliver 100% on time or even before time? Many times, in our daily rat race, we don't even look at this aspect. My urge to you is to at least look at it.

Change in Marketing Strategy

Marketing is one thing which is completely in your control. The easiest of all the other possibilities we have discussed. The more effective you are in marketing, the more direct impact you can see on your business growth. By the way, your sales team meeting customers for orders is not marketing. And yes, acknowledge it if you have not formally learned marketing. That's a good place to start, and then you can start to gain a better control over your business growth. We have already take it in a little more detail above in Part 2 of the book.

What change in equation do you plan to make?

____

____

____

____

____

Take The Next Step

Dear Readers,

As we reach the end of this book, I would like to express my deepest gratitude for taking the time to read this book.

This highly competitive world is full of opportunities. The export market offers high-profit margins and is more lucrative for most businesses. Imagine you have brought your business to its current level without much use of technology.

"Ambition is the first step to success, and second step is action".

You can plan a meeting with me over a cup of coffee to discuss how we can create a strategy and implement it step by step.

Together, let's make your export business even more successful!

You can connect with me at: **ng@thenextdesign.com**

Or

Ccontact me at: **98183 72742**

Warm Regards,

Nitin Gupta